MW00943602

in

Old Bottles

by Clayborn Huff

Table of Contents

Forward

Acknowledgements

Preface

Introduction

CHAPTERS

I

Forward *by Mark A Hardin*

Ten times in the book of Ecclesiastes the wise man, King Solomon, uses the word "vexation" to describe how he felt in his spirit when he looked around to see both the wonders of this earth, how its beauty was impossible to describe, and, how that man's working and toil seems to accomplish nothing.

Vexation is defined as "the state of irritation or annoyance". When the bus comes on time and we were one minute late because we had to run back to the car to grab our cell phone. We are at this point vexed! Something that just messes up our routine or day can become a vexation to our spirit, causing a disruption to our whole day.

This vexation of spirit awaits its chance to bite us when we begin to compare our way of thinking to that of the Word of God.

When we begin to delve into the Word of God we find that mankind has had a knack for dropping the ball at every opportunity God has given to be successful in Him. From the Garden of Eden to the Seven Churches in Revelations, we find time and time again where this human nature struggles with the will of God.

If Israel could have pursued Yahweh with all their heart, even during their failures, as King David did, then their earthly kingdom would have been established forever and would have never been moved. A continual, everlasting state of victory would have been there for the taking! Yet, the lure of idols seemed to be easier to pursue than trusting in a God that was invisible. It was easier to look around at other so-called religious people that seemed to have it all together and pick up their little nuances of religious formality.

Jesus, in Matthew 6:7, admonished that when we pray we should not use vain repetitions as the heathen. To pick up the mantras, repetitious prayers that the heathen would use for their gods, were not acceptable to Jehovah God. No matter how beautiful they sounded…even if they had stanzas that rhymed, had an excellent flow, and were music to the ears…Jesus said, don't pray to the Father using human terms. Ironically, the new birth experience would include an infilling of the Holy Spirit, accompanied with new (other) tongues. The old man's communication just didn't seem to fit when compared to the glorious experience of the Heavenlies!

Ezekiel chapter 20 addresses the issue of the children of Israel performing rituals of sacrificing their children to God, as those around them did to their gods. Though it may have seemed to be commendable that they wished to show their allegiance stronger than that of the heathen to their god, Yahweh rejected this form of worship.

"Wherefore say unto the house of Israel, Thus saith the Lord GOD; Are ye polluted after the manner of your fathers? and commit ye whoredom after their abominations? For when ye offer your gifts, when ye make your sons to pass through the fire, ye pollute yourselves with all your idols, even

III

unto this day: and shall I be enquired of by you, O house of Israel? As I live, saith the Lord GOD, I will not be enquired of by you. And that which cometh into your mind shall not be at all, that ye say, We will be as the heathen, as the families of the countries, to serve wood and stone."
(Ezekiel 20:30-32)

Interesting that the prophet would declare that everything that comes to mind won't be acceptable in the sight of God! We are creatures of habit, and those habits are influenced by all that surrounds us. Our five senses are enmity against God, so it seems. What we see, hear, smell, feel by touch, or taste has a powerful influence on what we think. To the point that we begin to think that God enjoys the same as we do. May I remind us that His ways are far above our ways, even past our finding out! Without the leading of the Spirit we cannot perceive the things of God.

As we follow Bro Clayborn Huff's thoughts in this book, I want to be the first to caution that our human spirit will not want to conform to the Word of God. It may even be a vexation at times.

There are many voices vying for your attention, and eventual worship. There is only One God that is worthy of your complete attention in worship. He is calling to a new life in Him...

ACKNOWLEDGEMENTS

All praise and honor, to the Author and finisher of this book; the Lord Jesus Christ. To the sons of God who are scattered all over this world, thanks to my wife Sissy who is the mother of my 5 smooth stones, Clay, Faith, Charity, Hope and Joy, who helped type and encourage me in writing this book. To Brother Mark Hardin who helped in his knowledge on how to arrange this book

Special thanks to my brothers, Rayborn, David Huff, and Keith Thibodeaux, for the many years on the road with David and the Giants, who not just spoke of the love of Christ but lived the life of Christ. To Christian Life Fellowship, in whom I've been honored to serve for over 25 years.

Clayborn Huff

PREFACE

Dear Reader,

The Lord woke me up early one morning with a word to write a teaching book. The Lord led me to the parable of the New Wine in old bottles, as I got into the parable; God gave me insight in what this reveals for the body of Christ. The church has a purpose for being here on earth, and until the purpose is revealed, the church will continue wondering around in the wilderness.

A word came to me over 20 years ago that said; Your main job is to set things in order; I believe this book is given by the Lord for the very purpose of setting his church in order, and I, who feels the least of the least, is this task given. I pray that everyone who reads this book will be pliable, and will be able to contain the new wine

Clayborn Huff

NEW WINE

CHAPTER 1

"And he spake also a parable unto them; no man putteth a piece of a new garment upon an old; if otherwise, then both the new maketh a rent, and the piece that was taken out of the new agreeth not with the old. And no man putteth new wine into old bottles; else the new wine will burst the bottles and be spilled, and the bottles shall perish. But new wine must be put into new bottles; and both are preserved. No man also having drunk old wine straightway desireth new: for he saith, The old is better." (Luke 5:36-39)

Matthew and Mark have this same parable. Evidently this foundational truth was most important for them to understand.

The new garment is Christ himself. The old garment can't move with the new, if the new is sowed on to the old, to patch a hole then when washed the new will change forms and make the hole worse. The new garment has to be attached to another new garment.

The old Adam nature of man is the old garment, there is no fixing or patching with anything new, it is born in sin and shapen in iniquity, the old garment can't receive anything from the new, it will only accept and move with what is old, for it to receive the new, the old has to die and be resurrected

1

"Knowing this, that our old man is crucified with him, that the body of sin might be destroyed, that henceforth we should not serve sin, for he that is dead is freed from sin." (Romans 6:6)

 The second part of the parable is that no man putteth new wine into old bottles, This was a common understanding of that day, that no man would put new wine in old wine skins, because they knew that the old wine skins would get set and when new wine would be put into an old set wine skin, the new wine would ferment and cause the old skins to burst and be spilled,

 New wine must be put into new wine skins. The new wine is the spirit of Christ that leads and guides his called out ones into all truth. The old man the flesh won't move with the spirit. He has his old school of theology, and can't or won't be led by the spirit, but will spill out what was given to him. New wine must be put into new wine skins. Old things must pass away, behold all things must be new.

"Therefore if any man be in Christ, he is a new creature: old things are passed away: behold all things are become new." (2 Corinthians 5:17)

 The old Adam nature of man can't be patched with new material, that which is flesh is fleshly and that which is spirit is spiritual, the Lord came to the earth to start a new creation, the old creation of man can't be fixed or repaired, it has to die.

"For the love of Christ constraineth us; because we thus judge that if one died for all, then were all dead, and that he died for all, that they which live should not henceforth live unto themselves, but unto him which died for them, and rose again."
(2 Corinthians 5:14-15)

We are a new creation in the Spirit, the flesh profits nothing.

No man also having drank old wine straightway desireth new, for he saith, the old is better. The carnal man is very proud of his much learning, he has set at the feet of the best teachers of his day, and has earned the title of "Doctor". The pharisaical religion had their schools and had very respectful teachers.

Paul was a Pharisee, who was very devout to the law of God and was persecuting the Christians who were filled with the new wine.

"I am verily a man which am a Jew, born in Tarsus, a city in Cilicia, yet brought up in this city at the feet of Gamaliel, and taught according to the perfect manner of the law of the fathers, and was jealous toward God, as ye all are this day and I persecuted this way unto the death, binding and delivering into prison both men and women."
(Acts 22:3-4)

After Paul's conversion, he became a new man. Everything he was taught was counted as nothing.

Paul was at first an old garment, and an old wine skin.

He was set and no man could change his mind. He felt that the law given to Moses was the truth and his religion was the only way, and the new teaching of Christianity was false. To him the old wine was better. The Lord appeared to Paul in a bright light that blinded his eyes (Acts 9:3-9). For three days he couldn't see and the Lord sent Ananias to pray for him. Paul received his sight and was filled with the Holy Ghost. He became a new wine skin, the old died in his conversion and baptism, he was resurrected to walk after the Spirit and to mortify the deeds of his sinful nature (Romans 6:4).

"There was a man of the Pharisees named Nicodemus, a ruler of the Jews. The same came to Jesus by night, and said unto him Rabbi, we know that thou art a teacher come from God; for no man can do these miracles that thou doest, except God be with him. Jesus answered and said unto him, verily, verily, I say unto thee, except a man be born again, he cannot see the kingdom of God. Nicodemus saith unto him, how can a man be born when he is old? Can he enter the second time into his mothers womb, and be born?"
(John 3:1-4)

Nicodemus knew that the miracles that Jesus was doing, couldn't be from man but had to be God with him. But Jesus wanted Nicodemus to see something greater than just the miracles, he wanted him to see the kingdom of God and the only way to truly see the kingdom, is to be born from above, "born anew."

These words were very confusing to Nicodemus, he couldn't understand how a man could enter back into his mother and be born again for the second time. Jesus said to him, except a man be born of water and of the Spirit, he cannot enter into the kingdom of God.

We don't enter back into the flesh, but rather enter into the Spirit, which allows us to enter into the kingdom of God. Jesus did many miracles, and that is a part of the kingdom of God but that's not what the kingdom is all about. Nicodemus came to see Jesus, because of the miracles which he saw and heard about. It didn't seem to impress Jesus that Nicodemus came to see him on that account.

The miracles were to get the attention of the people, so they could receive the teaching of the kingdom of God, and the only way to understand what Jesus was saying in his parables is to be born again.

The old nature of man, as wise as he may feel he is, can't understand the things of God because they are spiritually discerned. The Spirit reveals the Word. Without the Spirit we are none of his. For Nicodemus to receive the kingdom of God and be born again would cost him his place in this world system, He would be hated by his Pharisee religion and would lose his position as a ruler of the Jews. For him to do so, he would have to become as a new baby, and be taught all over again.

 Forgetting all of his much learning, and to be a new wine skin, this wouldn't come easy for a ruler of the Jews. His religion would turn their backs on him and call him deceived.

NEW WINE IN OLD BOTTLES

CHAPTER 2

"And said unto them , Thus it is written, and thus it behoved Christ to suffer, and to rise from the dead the third day: And that repentance and remission of sins should be preached in his name among all nations, beginning at Jerusalem. And ye are witnesses of these things. And, behold, I send the promise of my Father upon you: but tarry ye in the city of Jerusalem, until ye be undued with power from on high." (Luke 24:46-49)

The disciples did as Jesus told them to do, they were gathered together in an upper room praying, when suddenly there came a sound from Heaven as a rushing mighty wind, and it filled all the house where they were sitting, and they were all filled with the Holy Ghost , and began to speak with other tongues, as the spirit gave them utterance. The new wine was poured out on the disciples of Jesus, and for the new wine not to be wasted they would have to be flexible and willing to move with what the spirit would instruct them to do. This new wine they received has to be housed in new wine skins. The old wine skins of the traditions of men would hinder the move of the spirit of God.

"There were at Jerusalem Jews, devout men out of every nation under heaven, when this was noised abroad, the multitude came together, and were confounded, because that every man heard them speak in his own language." (Acts 2:5, 6)

"Others mocking said these men are full of new wine, but Peter, standing up with the eleven, lifted up his voice, and said unto them, Ye men of Judaea, and all ye that dwell at Jerusalem be this known unto you and harken to my words, for these are not drunken, as ye suppose, seeing it is but the third hour of the day., but this is that which was spoken by the prophet Joel, and it shall come to pass in the last days saith God, I will pour out of my spirit upon all flesh: and your sons and your daughters shall prophesy ,and your young men shall see visions, and your old men shall dream dreams." (Acts 2:13-17)

The parable that Jesus gave about the new wine, that it is to be put into new wine skins, was now put into his disciples. They in return would have to become born anew, old things will have to pass away all things will become new. They will have to go against their set ways of understanding God and the Law of Moses and be flexible to move with what the spirit is saying to the called out ones.

After Peter preached the word to the Jews they gladly received the word and were baptized, the same day about three thousand souls were added unto them. The church was being formed in righteousness, they continued steadfast in the apostles teaching and fellowship and praying together, many wonders and signs were done by the apostles.

"And all that believed were together, and had all things common" (Acts 2:44)

Israel was under the control of the Roman government. They were paying high taxes and suffering mental abuse from the Romans. Now under the new formed church, a Kingdom was being established inside a Kingdom. This Kingdom came without observation to the Romans, they couldn't see that King Jesus was on the throne of the hearts of this new formed church, and they were doing the same works Jesus did, when in his humanity. The devil will not allow the Kingdom to be set upon the earth without a fight, and he uses the old wineskins to withstand against the truth.

Peter and John went up together into the Temple to pray and there was a man who was lame and couldn't walk. Who ask them for some money, Peter said to him silver and gold have I none; but such as I have give I to you, in the name of Jesus Christ of Nazareth rise up and walk, and he leaping up stood, and walked, and entered with them into the Temple, walking, and leaping, and praising God. The people in the Temple were amazed at the miracle and they knew that it was he which sat for alms at the beautiful gate of the Temple; and they were filled with wonder and amazement at that which had happened unto him. Peter preached to them that Jesus was resurrected from the dead and in his name and faith in his name has made the lame man to walk. (Acts 3:16) And as they spake unto the people, the priests, and the captain of the temple, and the Sadducees, came upon them, being grieved that they taught the people, and preached through Jesus the resurrection from the dead.

These old wineskins were set in their ways, not even a miracle of God could convince them, that God was doing a new thing upon the earth, and for them to fight against this new thing, would be fighting against God, it would take a new birth, old things would have to die, but to them the old is better and this new thing couldn't be of God, for after all; if truth is to be given, it will have to come from our religion , for we hold on to the law of Moses, and have not forsaken the traditions of our forefathers, and if truth is to be given, it will have to come from our religion.

This type of mindset can never be molded into the new wineskins, even though some of these old wineskins can give in a little and receive the new wine, but when the spirit starts moving and goes against some of the traditions of men, then they want move with the spirit, both the wine is wasted and the old skins will burst and want be profitable to the Kingdom of God.

"Now when they saw the boldness of Peter and John, and perceived that they were unlearned and ignorant men, they marveled; and they took knowledge of them, that they had been with Jesus, and beholding the man which was healed standing with them, they could say nothing against it, but

*when they had commanded them to go aside out of
the council, they conferred among themselves,
saying, what shall we do to these men? For that
indeed a notable miracle hath been done by them
is manifest to all them that dwell in Jerusalem; and
we cannot deny it. But that it spread no further
among the people, let us straitly threaten them,
that they speak henceforth to no man in this name.
and they called them, and commanded them not to
speak at all nor teach in the name of Jesus. But
Peter and John answered and said unto them,
whether it be right in the sight of God to hearken
unto you more than unto God, judge ye, for we
cannot but speak the things which we have seen
and heard. After joining back with the believers,
they reported all that the chief priest and elders
had said to them, they prayed and the place was
shaken where they were assembled together; and
they were all filled with the Holy Ghost, and they
spake the word of God with boldness."*
(Acts 4: 13–20)

These new wineskins were being tested and
stretched, after praying they got some more of
Gods new wine.

For a new wineskin there has to be an acceptance,
that the inner life has full control, to mold and
move us in whatever direction that he so desires,
Humanity has made some bad mistakes, in
thinking they have God all figured out, in what is
pleasing to Him, when a man can say that he can
see, when the Lord hasn't opened his eyes to see,

then that man is blind. God has been in a process through the ages to bring humanity to a place to where he has purposed in himself from the foundation of the world, it is time for Gods children to come to revelation knowledge of His will for the world. It is a secret plan of God, and no man knows exactly how the end time will unfold, but for sure it will come differently than how man has figured it out, to be.

Peter was a very devoted man to the law, that God gave to Moses, for him to break these laws would be a great sin , from a young age he was taught in the law, of certain animals that were forbidden for the Jews to eat. They were also a very separated people, from the Gentiles, they had no dealings with them, and it was forbidden for them to go inside their houses. The time had come for a great change for the Jewish people, this would take a new wineskin without any trace of the old. This would be a stretching of faith and trust in God. The new wine in old bottles would surely burst, when the new thing of Gods plan is revealed, and it goes against their religion. To the Jewish people, their inheritance goes back to Abraham, Isaac and Jacob, of whom God chose as a chosen people out of the world, the Gentile or heathen people were without hope of being a part of the inheritance, but Gods plan was not revealed until the set time. When the law was given to the Israelites by Moses, to them, that was the whole truth; we have it; God gave it to us and our children and the world is lost, and we are the only ones that are pleasing to God, this was their thoughts from generation to generation, and no man would be able to convince them otherwise. Only a new birth and a new wineskin would be able to accept that God has in mind to graft the Gentile people into the inheritance with the Israelites, one new man in Christ.

"There was a certain man in Caesarea called Cornelius, a centurion of the band called the Italian band. A devout man ,and one that feared God with all his house, which gave much alms to the people, and prayed to God always. He saw in a vision evidently about the ninth hour of the day an angel of God coming in to him, and saying unto him, Cornelius. And when he looked on him, he was afraid, and said, What is it, Lord? And he said unto him, Thy prayers and thine alms are come up for a memorial before God. And now send men to Joppa, and call for one Simon, whose surname is Peter. He lodgeth with one Simon a tanner, whose house is by the sea side; he shall tell thee what thou oughtest to do. And when the angel which spake unto Cornelius was departed, he called two of his household servants, and a devout soldier of them that waited on him continually; and when he had declared all these things unto them, he sent them to Joppa. On the morrow, as they went on their journey, and drew nigh unto the city, Peter went up upon the housetop to pray about the sixth hour; And he became very hungry, and would have eaten; but while they made ready, he fell into a

*trance. And saw heaven opened, and a certain
vessel descending unto him, as it had been a great
sheet knit at the four corners, and let down to the
earth; wherein were all manner of fourfooted
beasts of the earth, and wild beasts, and creeping
things, and fowls of the air. And there came a
voice to him, Rise, Peter; kill, and eat. But Peter
said, not so, Lord; for I have never eaten any thing
that is common or unclean. And the voice spake
unto him again the second time, What God hath
cleansed, that call not thou common. This was
done thrice; and the vessel was received up again
into heaven. Now while Peter doubted in himself
what this vision which he had seen should mean,
behold, the men which were sent from Cornelius
had made enquiry for Simon's house, and stood
before the gate. And called, and asked whether
Simon, which was surnamed Peter, were lodged
there. While Peter thought on the vision, the Spirit
said unto him, Behold, three men seek thee. Arise
therefore, and go with them, doubting nothing; for
I have sent them."*   (Acts 10:1-20)

Peter doubted in himself about the vision, He
must to have thought; surely this vision was not
from God, because this goes against everything
that I have believed. And the scripture plainly
forbids eating anything common or unclean.

When Peter went and saw the men who came to
see him, it must have been a shock to him to see
those Gentile people. Who he had thought along
with the Jewish people; that the Gentile's were like

dogs; and that the Jews were the only Nation that God would be pleased with. This contradiction in his mind and heart could have been his greatest enemy, and not only his but for the rest of the whole world. Peter became pliable and stretched beyond his wildest imagination. The revelation; that Jews and Gentiles would become one body in Christ, would cause many Jews, that are set in old wineskins, to spill the new wine and burst. They will say; The old way is better and the Gentile people want keep the law of Moses, and they will defile the Temple of God.

Their faith was in their traditions, that they, felt were the only way to be of the truth. But Peter, as a new wineskin was willing to be stretched and led by the Spirit and went with the Gentile's to Cornelius house. (Acts 10: 28) He said unto them, ye know how that it is an unlawful thing for a man that is a Jew to keep company, or come unto one of another Nation, but God hath shewed me that I should not call any man common or unclean.

After Peter shared the word of God to the Gentiles, they received the gift of the Holy Ghost, and were baptized in the name of the Lord. This was a great blessing for the Gentile people, to be a part of the inheritance of the promises that was to Abraham and the children of Israel.

Not all of the Israelites were in agreement of the Gentile people being a part of the promises. Some of the Jews were teaching that the Gentile's would have to keep the laws of Moses, to be saved. The apostles had a meeting in regards to this, and decided through the inspiration of the Spirit, not to hold the Gentiles to the law, but to be led by the grace of God. To the old wineskins of religion, this was not the truth, so they persecuted the early church. (Acts 12: 1-3) Now about that time Herod the King stretched forth his hand to vex certain of the church, and he killed James the brother of John with a sword, and because he saw it pleased the Jews, he proceeded further to take Peter also. These were the days of unleavened bread.

  The early church was established with the teaching and life of Jesus Christ. They were rejected and called false teachers. In spite of the persecution of the Jews, the church grew in great number. Not only was the church a threat to the religion of the Jews, but also a threat to the Roman Government, who would fight them without mercy and against the Kingdom of God. These were the days of unleavened bread. The church wouldn't allow anything to come into the church that would bring them away from the truth; just a little leaven can rise to power and bring in a Pharisee religion, in an unleavened church.

"Ye did run well; Who did hinder you that ye should not obey the truth? This persuasion cometh not of him that called you. A little leaven leaveneth the whole church." (Galatians 5:7-9)

Jesus warns the disciples to beware of the leaven of the Pharisees, which is hypocrisy; Jesus said "FIRST OF ALL", so this was the first thing the early church would have to be on guard against. Hypocrisy is a deceitful and false truth, which seems to the natural man as the truth. But only the elect of God will be able to know truth and what is false. The false way will be so crafty, that Jesus said if it were possible, that even the elect could be deceived. But by his grace his children will hear the Sheppard's voice.

Paul was warned of God, that the leaven of hypocrisy would invade and rise to power.

"For I know this, that after my departing shall grievous wolves enter in among you, not sparing the flock; also of your own selves shall men arise, speaking perverse things, to draw away disciples after them. Therefore watch, and remember, that by the space of three years, I ceased not to warn every one night and day with tears, and now, brethren, I commend you to God, and to the word of his grace, which is able to build you up, and to give you an inheritance among all them which are sanctified." (Acts 20: 29-32)

Paul knew that his days on earth was coming to an end, and that the leaven of hypocrisy was going to be brought into the church, and it would rise to power, and the way of truth would be evil spoken of. Paul gave his last instructions in how to become an over comer in a perverse and crocked world. His instruction is this; To give yourself totally to the care and leadership of God, and to the word of his grace; by this we become back into the inheritance of the sons of God

"For as many as are led by the Spirit of God, they are the sons of God." (Romans 8:14)

So we can see that the early church, as powerful and anointed as they were, never came to the perfection that they strived to attain, they had to deal with carnal men, who desired to be justified by their own works, and not the grace of God.

"These be they who separate themselves, sensual, having not the spirit, but ye, beloved, building up yourselves on your most holy faith, praying in the Holy Ghost" (Jude 1: 19-20)

NO MAN PUTS A NEW GARMENT ON AN OLD ONE

CHAPTER 3

We can look at the history of Israel, that is recorded in the Old Testament and have an idea of how God has a plan, and is continuing to move in that direction to fulfill his will on the earth. After the fall of Adam and Eve, mankind lost fellowship with God and in their carnal minds tried to invent a god or gods that they could worship; They made gods of wood, that was overlaid with gold, some worshiped the sun and the stars, in whom the bible called, the gods they served devils,

The true God that created the world and all things, called Abraham and Sarah out of the pagan country, to establish a nation that would serve the true and living God.

Abraham and Sarah weren't able to have children, but for them to start a righteous Nation, they would have to have a son. So God promised to give a son to Abraham and Sarah. God blessed them with flocks, and herds, and silver, and gold. But the promise of a son seemed to be an impossibility to Sarah, because she was getting to old, in her mind, to have a son. So instead of waiting on the promise of God, she came up with her own plan.

"Now Sarai Abrams wife bare him no children, and she had an handmaid an Egyptian, whose

name was Hagar. And Sarai said unto Abram, behold now, the Lord hath restrained me from bearing, I pray thee, go in unto my maid, it may be that I may obtain children by her. And Abram hearkened to the voice of Sarai." (Gen 16: 1-2)

Hagar conceived and had a son, and his name was Ishmael. God appeared to Abraham and said, Sarah thy wife shall bear thee a son indeed, and you shall call his name Isaac and I will establish my covenant with him for an everlasting covenant, and with his seed after him. This was God's plan from the beginning, for Abraham and Sarah to bring forth a son of faith.

When mankind try's to help God out, by going against his will, then they will suffer for their wrong actions. The prophecy to Hagar before Ishmael was born was that God would multiply his children exceedingly, that it shall not be numbered for multitude. God promised to bless Ishmael because he was Abraham's son. But the downside to Ishmael is this;

"and he will be a wild man, his hand will be against every man, and every man's hand against him. And he shall dwell in the presence of all his brethren." (Genesis 16:12)

It is important to understand that God made no covenant with Ishmael but only to bless him. The covenant that God made was with Abraham and Isaac.

"And as for Ishmael, I have heard thee; Behold I have blessed him, and will make him fruitful, and will multiply him exceedingly; twelve princes shall he beget; and I will make him a great Nation. But my covenant will I establish with Isaac, which Sarah shall bear unto thee at this set time in the next year." (Genesis 17:20-21)

The covenant that God would establish with the promise son Isaac is that He would be his God, and the descents of Isaac would be a chosen people of God. But in order for the descent's to be a part of the covenant, they would have to follow the plan of God. The covenant that God made with Abraham is God making Abraham, not only the father of Isaac, but a father of many Nations. Through Isaac came one Nation, which are the Israelites, but the son in whom came the many Nations, is Christ Jesus. Abraham had the understanding, in the spirit, of a son of faith that would be born that would be the heir of the inheritance that was promised to Abraham's seed.

"Your father Abraham rejoiced to see my day; and he saw it, and was glad." (John 8: 56)

The apostle Paul had this revelation, that Jesus Christ is the seed of Abraham, in whom the inheritance of Abraham is fulfilled. Most of the Jewish people don't see the big picture; they only see the covenant of Isaac and not the covenant of Abraham.

God appeared to Abraham when he was 99 years old and made a covenant with him.

"and Abram fell on his face and God talked with him, saying. As for me, behold, my covenant is with thee, and thou shall be a father of many Nations. Neither shall thy name any more be called Abram, but thy name shall be Abraham; for a father of many nations have I made thee. And I will make thee exceeding fruitful, and I will make nations of thee, and Kings shall come out of thee. And I will establish my covenant between me and thee and thy seed after thee in their generation for an everlasting covenant, to be a God unto thee, and to thy seed after thee." (Genesis 17:3-7)

The covenants that God made with Abraham was for a future event, this word of prophesy was not for Isaac or Ishmael, it was for the coming Messiah. Through the covenant of Isaac's lineage the Messiah, Jesus Christ; would come, as the promise son of Abraham and the promise King, of the throne of David.

We will see through scripture that men will get a word from God, and will think that they have arrived at what pleases God; they make a religion around their new found faith, and worship that, as God. When Israel got the commandments from God, that Moses delivered to them, it was to them the end of the book; we are the chosen of God, we have his law, what more can we ask for, all we have to do, is keep his commandments and we will be the only ones on earth that is pleasing to God.

What they failed to see is that God is a progressive God, and he has a plan for the world and will not stop moving until it is accomplished.

Once these old wineskins get set and unmovable, then He will move on to others, who choose to follow the moving of the Spirit.

The Apostle Paul was of the religion of the Pharisees, who was very devout to the keeping of the Law of Moses, but after his conversion, he saw the light of revelation about the plan of God. It was totally contrary to what he was taught and believed. Paul knew in the Spirit that the just must live by faith, and not by the works of the law. The law was given to let the people know that sin is in the lives of all men and women, and that there is no good in any of them. But the new man is what Paul taught, to put on Christ, and put off the old nature of sin, and obey the law of the Spirit of life in Christ Jesus, who makes us free from the law of sin and death. As many as are led by the Spirit of Christ, they are the sons of the inheritance, who are, sons of God. Paul came to the place to where he turned from preaching to the Jews and turned to the Gentiles, because he saw that, no man puts a new garment on an old one. They were first called Christians at Antioch. This is where the grace of God was taught, and not to be justified by the works of the law, in which no man will be justified before God.

The grace of God is to abide in Christ, where He teaches us not to live ungodly in an ungodly world. The grace that is taught in most religions today, is a watered down grace, that teaches , to live ungodly in an ungodly world, by justifying sin, saying it's all covered under the blood. But Paul taught no such doctrine as that.

"What shall we say then? Shall we continue in sin, that grace may abound? God forbid. How shall we, that are dead to sin, live any longer therein?" (Romans 6:1-2)

"And the children struggled together within her, and she said, if it be so, why am I thus? And she went to enquire of the Lord and the Lord said unto her, two nations are in thy womb and two manner of people shall be separated from thy bowls; and the one people shall be stronger than the other people; and the elder shall serve the younger. And when her days to be delivered were fulfilled, behold there were twins in her womb. And the first came out red, all over like an hairy garment and they called his name Esau, and after that came his brother out, and his hand took hold on Esau's heel; and his name was called Jacob; and Isaac was threescore years old when she bare them." (Genesis 25:22-26)

   As we look through the bible, you began to understand that there are two types of people, one is after the blessing that comes from above, and the other is after the flesh, the carnal nature of man; who always wants to be in control. The flesh will fight against the spiritual minded people of God. Before the twins were born, there was a fight going on inside the mother, it was as if they knew, that the firstborn son would get the inheritance of Abraham. Esau came out first but when Jacob came out he had his hand on Esau's heel, which meant that Jacob wouldn't give up. The flesh was stronger, but by the strength of the Lord, Jacob would win the battle. In all rights, according to the ways of God, the firstborn son is heir to the inheritance, but the promise is by faith and not by the will of man, but by Gods divine choosing. He saw the desire of Jacob to have the blessing of God in his life, but Esau didn't see the importance of the inheritance and sold his birthright to Jacob.

Adam in like manner was the first son of God, but he was born of the earth, and through the fall, sold his birthright, to the devil. Through the fall of the first Adam all mankind were sold under sin, to the god of this world, but through the second Adam we have been redeemed from the curse.

As Jacob followed after the will and plan of God, and became pleasing in the sight of God, He changed Jacob's name to Israel. Gods plan from the beginning is starting to be revealed, little by little.

He chose Abraham and Sarah, with a promise of the earth covered with their offspring, now he chose Jacob to be a nation, which is called Israel that would serve the one true God, of Abraham, and Isaac. Israel had 12 sons; they grew in number and strength of the Lord. But God had another plan, for his chosen people to go into slavery to the

Egyptians, for the purpose to show other nations, that the God of Israel is God, and there is no other God besides Him.

In time God brought Israel out, to bring them into the promise land. To get to the promise land, there has to be a wilderness experience, in order to learn to trust someone that they didn't know. Many committed fornication, and God became angry with them and destroyed many of them. The gods in Egypt wasn't anything like the true God. He was holy and expected them to be holy also. God gave Moses the commandments, written on a stone, which represented the heart of the Israelites, who would keep the law to the best of their ability, but wouldn't have a heart of flesh, that would have compassion, and to be molded into the image of God.

KINGSHIP BEING FIRST REVEALED

CHAPTER 4

After Israel entered into the promise land, later they wanted a King over them just as other nations, have kings over them, that instruct, and govern their affairs. The prophet Samuel was grieved that they requested to have a king over them; he went to the Lord with their request.

"And the Lord said unto Samuel, hearken unto the voice of the people in all that they say unto thee; for they have not rejected thee, but they have rejected me, that I should not reign over them." (1 Samuel 8:7)

Gods plan for Israel is that He wanted to be their God and to govern and reign over them; He would be their defense against their enemy's. But the people saw Samuel getting older, and his sons were doing evil things. Samuel was their prophet, which God used to speak to the people. Their faith was not in God, who brought them to the promise land, through his own strength, and was well able to change the hearts of Samuel's sons, or to replace them with someone else. But God gave them their king, who was Saul, but he was self-willed, and was not under the obedience of God, but was a pleaser of man, and not a pleaser of God. He was rejected and David was chosen, as the King of Israel, a man that was after the heart of God, to obey and carry out his will on earth, as it is in Heaven. After David's death his son Solomon became King of Israel, but he allowed pagan worship to be accepted among the people. After David's death there would be good and bad Kings, the Kingship never had a King that was after the heart of God, as David was. But God had a plan to have a King like David, but greater, and this King would be King forever.

"And behold, thou shalt conceive in thy womb, and bring forth a son, and shall call his name Jesus. He shall be great, and shall be called the son of the Highest; and the Lord God shall give unto him the throne of his father David, and he shall reign over the house of Jacob for ever; and of his Kingdom there shall be no end." (Luke 1:31-33)

King David while living desired to build God a house to dwell in, but the word came to David, from God. "I will build you a house" Solomon built a house of God, but he confessed that the heaven of heavens can't contain God. But the true house of God was constructed by Jesus, he said tear this Temple down and in 3 days I will raise it back up, he was speaking of his body as the Temple of God, on the 3rd day he raised it from the dead, and we which believe are raised up with him.

"For if we have been planted in the likeness of his death, we shall be also in the likeness of his resurrection; knowing this, that our old man is crucified with him, that the body of sin might be destroyed, that henceforth we should not serve sin." (Romans 6:5-6)

So the plan of God is now revealed to those who have ears to hear, what the Spirit of God is saying to the called out ones of Christ.

Abraham's son that would be in great number, as the stars in heaven, are fulfilled, in Abraham's faith son Jesus Christ. Remember, the natural man will not understand what is being said, but will take a truth and corrupt it for their own profit or gain, and will lead others from Gods plan.

Not only is Jesus called the seed, or son of Abraham, but also the son of David, and the son of God. He is the son of Abraham for being the fulfillment of Gods promise to Abraham, to give him a son, as many as the stars above, this is in relation to the body of Christ, which is the church of the living God. Jesus was called the son of David, for a reason, Israel was looking for the Messiah to come and to set up the kingdom, Jesus was the King, but they didn't understand Gods plan for the Kingdom. His kingship is not of the world order, it's in the Spirit. God brought it back around to where he wanted it in the first place, and that is where He reigns and rules in the Spirit. He spoke in times past through his prophets, but now He is speaking through his sonship, the body of Christ.

Jesus is called the son of God; Adam is also called the son of God, by Adam and Eve's disobedience, they invited the devil and sin into the world, and it passed on to their children, from

generation to generation. But God had a plan to
start another sonship, through his only begotten
son Jesus Christ. Adam was made of the earth, but
the second Adam came from above. So the new
creation has to be born from above, God himself
being our Father. No man could have thought of a
better plan, no flesh can boast of their good works.
When grafted into Christ, we put on Christ and put
off the old Adam nature, giving it to the cross
daily.

   The plan of God has been fought by the devil to
bring the truth to a manmade religion. Most
churches believes the Kingdom of God will be set
up in the future, after the rapture, "as they call it"
but the prophesy of Jesus, is that he would set on
the Throne of David, and of his Kingdom there
shall be no end. King David's throne was on earth,
so for Jesus to be over the Kingship of his father
David, the Kingdom has to be on earth. God
honored his word from the Old Testament in rising
up a King to be over the house of Israel.

*"And when thy days be fulfilled, and thou shall
sleep with thy fathers, I will set up thy seed after
thee, which shall proceed out of thy bowels, and I
will establish his Kingdom, He shall build an
house for my name, and I will establish the throne
of his Kingdom for ever. I will be his father and he
shall be my son, if he commits iniquity, I will
chasten him with the rod of men, and with the
stripes of the children of men, but my mercy shall
not depart away from him, as I took it from Saul,*

whom I put away before thee. And thine house and thy Kingdom shall be established for ever before thee; thy throne shall be established for ever."
(2 Samuel 7:12-16)

This prophesy was to King David of a King that would come from his lineage, this prophesy was fulfilled in Luke chapter 1: 2. Jesus is the King of the Kingdom of God, but some will say, the Kingdom will come one day; but Jesus said the Kingdom is within you, and the Kingdom comes without the natural eye seeing it.

The Kingdom message is being preached today, but many preach it as a new religion, or for their own selfish gain, and not for the purpose, for the King to rule his own Kingdom. Thy Kingdom come, thy will be done, on earth, as it is in Heaven. Jesus gave a parable of how the Kingdom would come.

"Verily, verily, I say unto you, except a corn of wheat fall into the ground and die, it abideth alone, but if it die, it bringeth forth much fruit. He that loveth his life shall lose it; and he that hateth his life in this world shall keep it unto life eternal, if any man serve me. Let him follow me; and where I am, there shall also my servant be; if any man serve me, him will my Father honor."
(John 12:24-26)

The corn of wheat that Jesus is talking about is his body being put in the ground but through the resurrection, there was much wheat that the single seed produced, He brought much fruit into the Kingdom on the day of Pentecost, when the church was born from above. Once the King comes into the believer, then they are under another lordship, they have to hate their old life style and become under a new master, before coming to the Lord, we were our own master, and we can't call Him Lord or master without his Spirit. The King expects complete obedience in what He wants and desires of his servants. Jesus is the head of the church and the believers is his body; we are to carry out the finish work of Christ, until all things are subdued back under the control of the Spirit of God.

Some will say when Jesus comes back then he will set up the Kingdom, but Jesus said that he would be with us until the very end. The church, as a whole, is not laboring with him, in the Kingdom, because they are misled by the enemy, in taking the word of God naturally and not seeking his purpose and will for the world. Paul taught that we are in the Kingdom of Christ, and he was shown by God, what will happen when the end does come.

"then cometh the end, when he shall have delivered up the Kingdom to God, even the Father; when he shall have put down all rule and all authority and power. For he must reign, till he hath put all enemies under his feet. The last enemy that shall be destroyed is death. For he hath put all things under his feet. But when he saith all things

*are put under him, it is manifest that he is
expected, which did put all things under him ,and
when all things shall be subdued unto him, then
shall the Son also himself be subject unto him that
put all things under him, that God may be all in
all."*   (1 Corinthians 15:24-28)

The scripture plainly states that the Kingdom will
end when all things are subdued to Christ, and the
last enemy is death. He must reign till he hath put
all enemies under his feet. The mystery is; how is
he going to bring this about? Is he going to come
down from heaven and put down all rule and
authority? By judgment or is he going to use his
saints to bring this about. 1 Corinthians 15: 27
states, *"For he hath put all things under his feet."*
But when he saith all things are put under him, it is
manifest that he is expected, which did put all
things under him. Paul explains what he meant by
all things are put under his feet.

*"And hath put all things under his feet, and gave
him to be head over all things to the church, which
is his body, the fullness of him, that filleth all in
all."* (Ephesians 1:22-23)

When Israel came out of Egypt into the
wilderness, they were to go into the promise land
and set up a nation ruled by God. In like manner
the Kingdom of the church has to be under
Heavens Government.
   The Government of this world is trying to set up a
new world order, but this is Satan's plan to take

control of the whole world, and to overthrow the Kingdom of Christ. But God has a plan and the outcome of this plan is found in Daniel chapter 7:

"I beheld, and the same horn made war with the saints, and prevailed against them; until the ancient of days came, and judgment was given to the saints of the Most High; and the time came that the saints possessed the Kingdom."
(Daniel 7:21-22)

"And the Kingdom and dominion, and the greatness of the Kingdom under the whole heaven shall be given to the people of the Saints of the Most High, whose Kingdom is an everlasting Kingdom, and all dominions shall serve and obey him." (Daniel 7:27)

This prophesies shows that the church will go through percussion until the very end. But judgment and power will be given to the Saints of God. Let this be understood by the church, the judgment that God will send to the world through the church will not be through violence, those who live by the sword will die by the sword. Jesus said my Kingdom is not of this world, if it were then my servants would fight. The Kingdom of God is from above, so the judgment of the world will come from above, but God will use his church, the body of Christ to warn the world. In Revelation 11: 1-14 the two witnesses prophesy as the Spirit empowers them, they are killed, but God resurrected them, a great earthquake kills many by

Gods judgment; after this, it says in Revelations 11: 15, *"And the seventh angel sounded, and there were great voices in heaven, saying The Kingdoms of this world are become the Kingdom of our Lord and of his Christ, and he shall reign for ever and ever."*

  Let this be understood by the called out ones. Jesus Christ is still the same yesterday, today, and forever. What he was yesterday walking with his disciples, He is now in his called out ones, walking with the body of Christ in the Spirit.

NEW WINE WILL BURST THE BOTTLES

CHAPTER 5

When the church was filled with the new wine in the book of Acts chapter 2, they were led and taught by the Spirit of truth, these Jewish believers didn't have the revelation at this time that the God of the Israelites was also going to be the God of the Gentiles as well.

Once the Gentiles were grafted into the new found faith of Christianity, most devout Jews rejected the idea that the Gentiles would be of the same inheritance with them. Percussion arose from the Pharisee religion. Some of the new Jewish believers couldn't receive such a change, because it went against their traditions and also they were prejudice against the Gentile people. Many couldn't be led by the Spirit, and their bottles couldn't hold the new wine of the Spirit.

The persecution was not just from the Jewish religion but also from the Gentile Nation, who was devout to their religion, they worshiped many gods, and had statues that were worshiped as well. Christianity was a threat to their culture and would hurt them that made money from making these idols.

"Moreover ye see and hear, that not alone at Ephesus, but almost throughout all Asia, this Paul hath persuaded and turned away much people, saying that they be no gods, which are made with

hands. So that not only this our craft is in danger to be set at naught; but also that the Temple of the great goddess Diana should be despised, whom all Asia and the world worshippeth and when they heard these sayings, they were full of wrath, and cried out, saying great is Diana of the Ephesians." (Acts 19:26-28)

The early church went through great persecution for the name of the Lord. Many were killed and suffered many things for the Kingdom of God, but they didn't fight back but put all judgment into Gods hands. But Satan couldn't stop the spread of Christianity.

The devil is wiser than people give him credit. He knows the things that are to come, so he sets up false religions that will look right to a natural minded man, and they would become so dedicated to this religion that some would offer their children as a sacrifice to this false god. Which is the devil deceiving the simple minded people.

The devil first deceived Adam and Eve, and then he set up a false religion, so that he would be worship as God, knowingly by some and unknowingly by many, his goal was to kill, still, and destroy, the lives of humanity. The Ephesian people were worshiping these false gods, which goes all the way back to the worship of Baal and the tower of Babel. It spread into Egypt and into the entire world.

These religions are argued by some, that they were before Christianity, so they must be the true religion, even if they did wicked things. But their thinking is wrong; the first was Adam and Eve, God walked with them and was their every need. Satan came afterward and started his religion, so that he could be worshiped as God, this was his goal from the beginning. But the second Adam, Jesus Christ restored the sons of God back to himself, to the true and living God.

I don't expect the intellect man, atheist, or natural man to understand the working of God and the tricks of the evil one, Paul said, we're not ignorant of his devices, the secrets of God are revealed to the Spiritual man not to the carnal man.

The Lord gave a word of prophecy after the fall of Adam and Eve;

"and I will put enmity between thee and the woman, and between thy seed and her seed; it shall bruise thy head and thou shalt bruise his heel." (Genesis 3:15)

God said he would put enmity between the seed of the woman and the devils seed. Many will agree that the scripture is speaking of Jesus Christ born of a virgin; the Adam nature of man had nothing to do with the birth of Christ. Jesus would bruise the head of Satan in taking away his authority upon Gods people; Satan would have an attack on the church but only to bruise the hill.

There will be enmity between the seed of the woman, which is Christ, and the seed of the Adam nature.

"For to be carnal minded is death; but to be spiritually minded is life and peace, because the carnal mind is enmity against God; for it is not subject to the law of God, neither indeed can be. So then they that are in the flesh cannot please God." (Romans 8:6-8)

The enmity between the woman's seed and the devils seed is the carnal mind; the natural man has the pride of his intellect. The desire for knowledge that Eve desired is passed on down to Adam and Eves children.

Revelation knowledge is good, but when knowledge comes from the natural man about spiritual things, then you will know that the devils hand is in on it, the word of God has the final word, and it is the truth, everything else comes from the father of lies.

You may ask, can confessed Christians be of the wrong seed? Yes; this is the first place the devil will try to deceive. The world without Christ are already deceived and led astray, Jesus said, many in the day of judgment will confess him, but Jesus will confess to never knowing them, they evidently thought they knew him, but must have known the evil one instead. Who can transform himself as an angel of light.

Jesus came to his own people that were of the promise seed of Abraham, who were praying for the Messiah, "Christ" to come. They had their own intellect of how, and where, the Christ would come. Even though he did signs and wonders they called him false because he didn't line up to their knowledge that came from the natural man. The carnal man with his religion, became prideful, not knowing; that of his much accomplishments that he had replaced God with his head knowledge about God and not seeking for truth, which only comes from above. Jesus came for the purpose to redeem man back to a communion with God, and this communion only comes through the new creation of the sonship of Jesus Christ.

The law was given to let the people know what was required of them as to the sinful nature of mankind, but the law was not the answer to fix the problem, it only let them know that they were in bondage to the wicked one the devil.

"Then said Jesus to those Jews which believed on him, if ye continue in my word, then are ye my disciples indeed; and ye shall know the truth, and the truth shall make you free. They answered him, we be Abrahams seed, and were never in bondage to any man; how sayest thou ye shall be made free? Jesus answered them, verily, verily, I say unto you; whosoever committeth sin is the servant of sin. And the servant abideth not in the house for ever; but the son abideth ever." (John 8:31-35)

Have you ever wondered why there are so many denominations in Christianity? And every one of them believes that they are the true church. I've studied church history and believe God has given me an understanding in this. Know this for sure, God is in control and that in due time he will bring everything under his dominion. When the early church began in the first century, there were already false prophets going out into the world preaching a false Christianity, which was contrary to the teaching of the Apostles, John called them Anti-Christ.

"Little children it is the last time; and as ye have heard that antichrist shall come, even now are there many antichrist; whereby we know that it is the last time; They went out from us, but they were not of us; for if they had been of us, they would no doubt have continued with us; but they went out, that they might be made manifest that they were not all of us. But ye have unction from the Holy one, and ye know all things." (1 John 2:18-20)

From the start there were two types of Christians, the Spirit lead and the carnal man, who was not under the unction (anointing) from God, but were led by their carnal minds, these left the early church and formed their own religious order. They were called antichrist because Christ was not in them, they had a form of godliness, but denied his authority in their lives,

"For as many as are led by the Spirit of God, they are the sons of God." (Romans 8:14)

The early church apostles wrote letters to the one true church warning them to be on guard against the false teachings that were being preached.

"For I am jealous over you with godly jealousy; for I have espoused you to one husband, that I may present you, as a chaste virgin to Christ but I fear, lest by any means, as the serpent beguiled Eve through his subtilty, so your minds should be corrupted from the simplicity that is in Christ, For if he that cometh preaching another Jesus, whom we have not preached, or if ye receive another spirit, which ye have not received, or another gospel, which ye have not accepted, ye might well bear with him." (2 Corinthians 11:2-4)

Paul was saying that he and the Apostles had laid the right foundation in leading them to the truth, which was Christ in them the hope of glory and the word which was able to save their souls.

The devil had a plan to destroy Christianity all together, the Apostles were killed and put in prison, and their letters were burned and destroyed, without the letters the world wouldn't know what true Christianity was all about. But there were Christians who copied the letters from the Apostles who hid the letters in caves, and different places. They were amazingly found, and these letters make up the New Testament that we treasure today; The persecution lasted for a long time, but Christianity spread all over, and also into Rome, the Romans worshiped many gods, the sun and the host of heaven was worshiped, this religion goes back to Nimrod who had the tower of Babel built,

The Roman people were very devout to their religion and persecuted the Christians. After the Emperor Constantine was converted to Christianity he made it the State religion in Rome, after this the persecution stopped, by the Roman Government.

It couldn't have been an easy transition for the Emperor Constantine to convince the Roman people to give up their religion, so a lot of their pagan beliefs were adopted into the Catholic church.

The Romans worshiped a goddess, so the worship of Mary could have been a way for the church to please the Romans. Whatever the reason of this fable, it's just not a part of the Christian Faith that the Apostles taught. The whole concept of the Catholic Church is not based on the word of God but on the structure of the Roman Government.

Christ Jesus is the head of the Church, One of the Popes titles is Vicar of Christ, Vicar means a person in the place of someone, when he is absent, Martin Luther said; if the Pope is in the place of Christ, then this is the spirit of antichrist.

In 325AD the Emperor Constantine called for the Counsel of Nicaea, there was division in the Catholic church about the deity of Jesus so they came up with the creed of the trinity doctrine and other issues; "which is the creed also of the Protestant churches ". All that taught contrary to the Catholic church would be considered false, many were put in prison or burned at the stake. The common people were forbidden to have the word of God. Only the Priest could interpret the word of God, which was against the word, which says; all will be taught by God.

The reformation is credited to Martin Luther, but others before Luther saw corruption in the Catholic Church, one was John Hus who tried to warn them of their errors but they had him burned at the stake, he lived one hundred years before Luther. John Wycliffe, William Tyndale was also persecuted for standing for the word of God; William Tyndale was also burned at the stake for truth.

Martin Luther was a teacher in the Catholic church, but he also saw through scripture that what was being taught by the Catholic church was not scriptural, one of the teachings was the selling of Indulgences, which the common people were told that they could pay money to get their love ones that died out of Purgatory, this was a place that was taught, that was like hell. Luther knew that through scripture that Jesus Christ paid the price himself on the cross, and you can't buy your way into heaven.

The Catholic Church brought Luther to trial, and would have had him killed, but the German people protected Luther, he was taken to a castle for his safety, while there he translated the bible into the German language. This was the beginning of the many denominations in the world. Each denomination was founded on a truth or something their carnal minds thought was the truth. Some thought by worshiping on a certain day was the truth that was missing, some don't have music instruments, thinking their roots goes back to the first century church, but all these beliefs are carnal and far from Christianity; these are blind guides, which strain at a gnat, and swallow a camel; revelation knowledge is from God, but you don't make a religion out of it. Most of these religions are not for the love of God, but for the love of money and power.

The Catholic Church wants her children to come back to her, most all protestant churches, goes by the Catholic Church creed that was founded in 325AD. "What's wrong in letting the word of God being the only creed we are to live by? The Catholic Church believes that they are the true Church, that goes back to the first century, I believe their religion does go back to the first century and the word speaks of them or someone with the same spirit.

"Little children, it is the last time, and as ye have heard that antichrist shall come, even now are there many antichrist; whereby we know that it is

45

the last time, they went out from us, but they were not of us, for if they had been of us, they would no doubt have continued with us, but they went out, that they might be made manifest that they were not all of us." (1 John 2:18-19)

Jesus said by their fruit you shall know them, the fruit of the past is thieves and murders, who had the Government of Rome on their side. Her daughters the Protestant church has blood on their hands also. All the reformers of the past were in hopes of reforming the Roman church, but how can you reform a wrong structure? The bible does not call for a reform but rather to be transformed.

"And be not conformed to this world; but be ye transformed by the renewing of your mind, that ye may prove what is that good, and acceptable and perfect, will of God." (Romans 12:2)

What religion can say, we are the true religion? None of them; truth comes not through the precepts of man but rather knowing the Lord, knowing the truth will set you free, and what is truth? Jesus said it well;

"Jesus saith unto him, I am the way, the truth, and the life, no man cometh unto the Father, but by me. If ye had known me, ye should have known my Father also and from henceforth ye know him, and have seen him." (John 14:6-7)

The truth is the simplicity that is in Christ, where he leads and teaches his sons and daughters in his righteousness, and to love one another, and hate every false way. God has a plan for the body of Christ; the ones who are set in their old wineskins will not be able to expand with the moving of Gods Spirit, no man will glory in what he has accomplished in this life, all glory will go to the King of Kings, Lord of lords, Jesus the Christ;

"Having made known unto us the mystery of his will according to his good pleasure which he hath purposed in himself, that in the dispensation of the fullness of times he might gather together in one all things in Christ, both which are in heaven, and which are on earth; even in him; In whom also we have obtained an inheritance, being predestinated according to the purpose of him who worketh all things after the counsel of his own will; That we should be to the praise of his glory, who first trusted in Christ. In whom ye also trusted, after that ye heard the word of truth, the gospel of your salvation; in whom also after that ye believed, ye were sealed with that holy spirit of promise."
(Ephesians 1:9-13)

JUDGEMENT OF GOD

CHAPTER 6

I went to Jamaica once and was amazed at all the different religions that were there, each denomination sends their missionaries to a foreign country not to spread Christianity but to spread their religion, they have their tracks and try to convince the people to believe in their religion.

What happens is the country becomes divided, besides the love of God shed abroad in their hearts, they have a self-righteous attitude that has been imparted into them, and they can quote their pet scriptures that prove they are the only true ones of God. When they read the bible, it's not for the purpose of allowing the word to become a part of their lives but to search the scriptures to support their religion.

While in Jamaica we met this married couple who were confessed Christians who were converted to separate denominations, they were only permitted to go to the denomination that they belonged to, they were divided in their home and in their belief. This my friend is not true Christianity;

"But If we walk in the light, as he is in the light, we have fellowship one with another, and the blood of Jesus Christ his son cleanseth us from all sin." (John 1:7)

Two people can't walk together unless they are in agreement, so how can we come into agreement with one another? By abiding in the vine,

"I am the vine, ye are the branches; He that abideth in me, and I in him, the same bringeth forth much fruit; for without me ye can do nothing, if a man abide not in me, he is cast forth as a branch and is withered, and men gather them, and cast them into the fire." (John 15:5-6)

Many try to find the missing revelation in what pleases God, I have met a lot of different people in my Christian walk, that have come up with a lot of different ideas; one didn't believe in wearing shoes, some believe that the name of Jesus has to be on the church building, there are a lot of different works that people have sought after to be pleasing to God, but Jesus gives us the key in what work is pleasing to him;

"Then said they unto him, what shall we do, that we might work the works of God, Jesus answered and said unto them, This is the work of God, that ye believe on him whom he has sent."
(John 6:28-29)

To believe on him, is to believe in him, where he abides in us and we abide in him, to believe on the Lord is a much deeper word than what most religions understand it to mean. To believe is the same Hebrew word for" trust the Lord"

The Israelites when coming out of Egypt believed in the Lord, but through the temptation in the wilderness didn't trust the Lord and didn't enter into the promise land. To trust the Lord, is to not trust in your own work, but to allow him to be master and Lord of your life, where he clothes you with his righteousness. In Revelation 3:17 the church is found naked, but they confessed to have everything that was needed, they were as Adam and Eve they clothed themselves when the presence of God had left them. A part of the inheritance of Christ, is that he clothes us with himself. God clothed Adam and Eve with a sacrificial animal, the church in Revelation were naked by their own works. Their spirits were naked and in need of being clothed in the spirit of Christ, where they are to be clothed in his righteousness. Our righteousness is filthy rags in his sight.

Jesus gave two laws for the church to live by, to love God with all our heart, mind, body, and soul, and the other, to love your neighbor as you love your own self. The law and the prophets are fulfilled in these two laws.

You may ask does not the revelation of the cross, baptism, and other doctrines matter. Of course it does, but all revelation knowledge only points to the truth. These are our elementary truths to bring faith into our hearts, but when these elementary truths become the truth, then growth stops at that level.

Paul pressed toward the mark of a higher calling and leaving the elementary teaching, and going on into perfection.

"Therefore leaving the principles of the doctrine of Christ, let us go on unto perfection; not laying again the foundation of repentance from dead works, and of faith toward God, of the doctrine of baptisms, and of laying on of hands, and of resurrection of the dead, and of eternal judgment." (Hebrews 6:1-2)

So what is perfection, and how do we get there? Perfection is full maturity in Christ? Perfection is what every minister of the word of God should be teaching.

"for the perfecting of the saints; for the work of the ministry , for the edifying of the body of Christ; till we all come in the unity of the faith, and of the knowledge of the son of God, unto a perfect man, unto the measure of the stature of the fullness of Christ; that we henceforth be no more children, carried about with every wind of doctrine, by the sleight of men, and cunning craftiness, whereby they lie in wait to deceive; but speaking the truth in love, may grow up into him in all things, which is the head, even Christ." (Ephesians 4:12-15)

Some will say "I know that I'll never be perfect, there was only one that was perfect". That statement is true and false, the perfection that we are to achieve is not our own perfection but rather allowing the perfect one to be Lord of our lives. As Paul said, it is no longer I but Christ within.

Growing up into Christ is a process that begins when one is born again, the Spirit of Christ, through love will reveal the evilness of our nature. As we pick up our cross to follow his leadership, we die daily to anything and everything that is not pleasing to the inner life. When any action that is done, that is not pleasing to the inner life, there will be a quenched spirit within. A son of God will be very sensitive, and will know when the Spirit is offended with him. Repentance brings back the fellowship with the spirit within. As we grow in Christ, allowing him his authority as the head of our spiritual body, and our natural body dead to sin and the world, the perfection of the body of Christ will be manifest to the world, that Christ is come in the flesh.

"Hereby know ye the Spirit of God; Every Spirit that confesseth that Jesus Christ is come in the flesh is of God; and every spirit that confesseth not that Jesus Christ is come in the flesh is not of God; and this is that spirit of antichrist, whereof ye have heard that it should come, and even now already is it in the world." (1 John 4:2-3)

The antichrist is the natural man who fights against the existence of a "Messiah" Christ who lives in the saints of the called out ones. The antichrist are of the world system, and the world relates to their carnal beliefs, but those of faith

52

have overcome them because greater is he that is within them than those in the world.

The Lord woke me up with a word awhile back that said "The god of this world took control of the sons of God". People of this world have no idea of how cleaver and deceiving the devil, the god of this world, really is. He has used religion as a cover of his deceit. As the serpent beguiled Eve through his subtility, so has he corrupted the minds of the sons of God, from the simplicity that is in Christ. The word simplicity means singleness and not self-seeking.

Let it be understood, all that led people from the indwelling Christ are false prophets. Whether they call themselves Pope, Joseph Smith, latter day saints, Jehovah Witness, Mohammed religion, which is Islam. I can't name them all the list goes on and on of these self –seeking men. The sons of God are in Babylonian captivity, but the Lord knows who are his, and he can bring them out unto himself. They will hear the voice of the Shepherd and will not know the voice of a stranger, the Lord will prevail;

God at different times would allow Israel to go into bondage because they served other gods and were influenced by the world, but when they prayed and turned their hearts to him, he would forgive and bring them out unto himself. It's not Gods will for his children to perish, or "to be in darkness". God is love and the foundation of the life of Jesus Christ was love and compassion for a lost world, his strongest rebuke was not to the woman caught in adultery, but to the Pharisaical religion for their pride and arrogant behavior. Jesus showed the real heart of God, and it's all based around one thing, Love;

These religions who have killed others for their religion has killed for a false god, his name is Satan.

"In this the children of God are manifest, and the children of the devil; whosoever doeth not righteousness is not of God, neither he that loveth not his brother. For this is the message that ye heard from the beginning, that we should love one another, not as Cain, who was of that wicked one, and slew his brother, and wherefore slew he him? Because his own works were evil, and his brothers righteous." (1 John 3:10-12)

The world as a whole, haven't seen true Christianity. They have seen religion, with all the misfits on television, who practiced sin before the whole world, to bring a reproach to the name of Christ. Catholic priests abusing children. Rome paying the bill for the law suits, placing them in different locations, when they should be behind bars. Is not God angry with this system of Satan? Yes he is, there has to be repentance, a change of heart, God does forgive, but there has to be a change in the thinking of these religions. Better to answer to God now, than to stand before him on the day of judgment, thinking that eating the cracker and drinking the wine is your assurance of heaven. Many will be shocked when he says depart from me I never knew you,

The Lord has been giving Jews and Moslems dreams and visions of himself, to bring them out unto himself; many of them are going through persecution for the name of Christ Jesus. I believe these could become some of the great men and women of God that can turn the world upside down. I pray they won't be influenced with the religions of our day, but will be led by the Spirit of Christ.

I pray that all religions will pray for truth, and not to be deceived or to deceive others.. From the least, to the greatest, all will be taught by God.